THE CHICKEN
COOKBOOK

Photography by Peter Barry
Designed by Richard Hawke and Claire Leighton
Edited by Jillian Stewart and Kate Cranshaw
Recipes by Judith Ferguson, Lalita Ahmed and
  Carolyn Garner

3446
© 1993 Coombe Books
This edition published in 1994 by Coombe Books for
Parragon Book Service Ltd
Unit 13-17, Avonbridge Trading Estate
Atlantic Road, Avonmouth, Bristol BS11 9QD
All rights reserved
Printed and bound in Hong Kong
ISBN 1-85813-356-4

THE CHICKEN
COOKBOOK

PARRAGON

Contents

Introduction

Chicken is one of the most popular meats eaten today. This is due, to a certain extent, to the large numbers of people who are eating less red meat in an attempt to reduce their fat and cholesterol intakes. In addition to being perfect for both healthy and low-calorie diets, chicken has the added advantage of being quick and easy to cook, as well as lending itself to a whole variety of cooking methods and complementary ingredients.

When choosing a fresh chicken, look at the skin, it should be pale and moist looking, and the breast meat should be plump. Make sure that the packaging is intact, so that the chicken hasn't been exposed to the air – this goes for frozen chicken as well. Fresh chicken should be removed from its packaging and kept covered, for no more than three days in the refrigerator. Frozen chicken should be thoroughly defrosted before using, and then cooked immediately. All chicken should be cooked from room temperature, but that does not mean that it should be left standing in the warm for a long time. When stuffing a chicken, do not pack the cavity too tightly, this will allow hot air to circulate round and ensure that it cooks thoroughly. Chicken should never be cooked from frozen or partially thawed and never be eaten pink or bloody.

As chicken is so popular, it can be bought in many forms; whole, quartered, or jointed – with or without bones. Although buying portions is convenient for the cook, it is expensive. It is much cheaper to buy a whole chicken and joint it yourself. Whole birds can also be bought as free-range or corn-fed (with a yellow tinted skin), and these have a very good flavour. Young chickens, known as poussins, are also readily available. Depending on their size, they will each feed one or two people and make a very neat and attractive dish. Whole birds can also be boned and stuffed for special occasions, or 'spatchcocked', by splitting in half lengthways up the underside and then flattening out on skewers. Boneless breast fillets are one of the most popular portions simply because they are so convenient for slicing, mincing and cutting into chunks.

With such a choice of cuts and cooking methods it is little wonder so many recipes for chicken exist. This book contains a variety of delicious recipes suitable for all occasions, and includes recipes from around the world, as well as more familiar starters and main courses. So, whether you want a dish for a cold winter's day, a dinner party, a lunch, or a Chinese meal, you need look no further than the recipes in this book.

CHICKEN SATAY

This typical Indonesian dish is very spicy, and makes an excellent starter.

SERVES 4

2 tbsps soy sauce
2 tbsps sesame oil
2 tbsps lime juice
1 tsp ground cumin
1 tsp turmeric powder
2 tsps ground coriander
450g/1lb chicken breast, cut into 2.5cm/
   1-inch cubes
2 tbsps peanut oil
1 small onion, very finely chopped
1 tsp chilli powder
120g/4oz crunchy peanut butter
1 tsp brown sugar
Lime wedges and coriander leaves, for
   garnish

1. Put the soy sauce, sesame oil, lime juice, cumin, turmeric and coriander into a large bowl and mix well.

2. Add the cubed chicken to the soy sauce marinade and stir well to coat the meat evenly.

3. Cover with cling film and allow to stand in a refrigerator for at least 1 hour, but preferably overnight.

4. Drain the meat, reserving the marinade.

5. Thread the meat onto 4 large or 8 small kebab skewers and set aside.

6. Heat the peanut oil in a small saucepan and add the onion and chilli powder. Cook gently until the onion is slightly softened.

7. Stir the reserved marinade into the oil and onion mixture, along with the peanut butter and brown sugar. Heat gently, stirring constantly, until all the ingredients are well blended.

8. If the sauce is too thick, stir in 2-4 tbsps boiling water.

9. Arrange the skewers of meat on a grill pan and cook under a preheated moderate grill for 10-15 minutes. After the first 5 minutes of cooking, brush the skewered meat with a little of the peanut sauce to baste.

10. During the cooking time turn the meat frequently to cook it on all sides and prevent it browning.

11. Garnish the satay with the lime and coriander leaves, and serve the remaining sauce separately.

TIME: Preparation takes about 25 minutes plus at least 1 hour marinating, cooking takes about 15 minutes.

SERVING IDEAS: Serve with a mixed salad.

9

Terrine of Spinach and Chicken

This superb terrine is ideal when you want to impress your guests with a delicious starter.

SERVES 6-8

225g/8oz chicken breasts, boned and
    skinned
2 egg whites
120g/4oz fresh white breadcrumbs
450g/1lb fresh spinach, washed
1 tbsp each of fresh finely chopped chervil,
    chives and tarragon
Salt and freshly ground black pepper
280ml/½ pint double cream
60g/2oz finely chopped walnuts
Pinch nutmeg

1. Cut the chicken into small pieces.

2. Put the cut chicken, 1 egg white and half of the breadcrumbs into a food processor. Blend until well mixed.

3. Put the spinach into a large saucepan and cover with a tight-fitting lid.

4. Cook the spinach for 3 minutes, or until it has just wilted.

5. Remove the chicken mixture from the food processor and rinse the bowl.

6. Put the spinach into the food processor along with the herbs, the remaining egg white and breadcrumbs. Blend until smooth.

7. Season the chicken mixture with a little salt and pepper and add half of the cream. Mix well to blend thoroughly.

8. Add the remaining cream to the spinach along with the walnuts and the nutmeg. Beat this mixture well to blend thoroughly.

9. Line a 450g/1lb loaf tin with greaseproof paper and lightly oil.

10. Pour the chicken mixture into the base of the tin and spread evenly.

11. Carefully pour the spinach mixture over the chicken mixture, and smooth the top with a palette knife.

12. Cover the tin with lightly oiled aluminium foil and seal this tightly around the edges.

13. Stand the tin in a roasting pan and pour enough warm water into the pan to come halfway up the sides of the tin.

14. Cook the terrine in a preheated oven 160°C/325°F/Gas Mark 3 for 1 hour, or until it is firm.

15. Put the terrine into the refrigerator and chill for at least 12 hours.

16. Carefully lift the terrine out of the tin and peel off the paper. To serve, cut the terrine into thin slices with a sharp knife.

TIME: Preparation takes 25 minutes, cooking takes 1 hour, refrigeration takes 12 hours.

SERVING IDEAS: Serve slices of the terrine on individual serving plates garnished with a little salad.

CHICKEN STUFFED PEPPERS

*Try a stuffing that is different from the usual meat and rice one
for lighter tasting peppers.*

SERVES 6

3 large green or red peppers
60g/2oz butter or margarine
1 small onion, finely chopped
1 stick celery, finely chopped
1 clove garlic, crushed
3 chicken breasts, skinned, boned and
  diced
2 tsps chopped parsley
Salt and pepper
½ loaf of stale bread, made into crumbs
1-2 eggs, beaten
6 tsps dry breadcrumbs

1. Cut the peppers in half lengthwise and remove the cores and seeds. Leave the stems attached, if wished.

2. Melt the butter in a frying pan and add the onion, celery, garlic and chicken. Cook over moderate heat until the vegetables are softened and the chicken is cooked. Add the parsley. Season with salt and pepper.

3. Stir in the stale breadcrumbs and add enough beaten egg to make the mixture hold together.

4. Spoon filling into each pepper half, mounding the top slightly. Place the peppers in a baking dish that holds them closely together.

5. Pour enough water around the peppers to come about 1.25cm/½ inch up their sides. Cover and bake in a pre-heated 180°C/350°F/Gas Mark 4 oven for about 45 minutes, or until the peppers are just tender.

6. Sprinkle each with the dried breadcrumbs and place under a preheated grill until golden brown.

TIME: Preparation takes about 30 minutes and cooking takes about 45-50 minutes.

VARIATIONS: Use spring onions in place of the small onion. Add chopped nuts or black olives to the filling, if wished.

SERVING IDEAS: Serve as a first course, either hot or cold, or as a light lunch or supper with a salad.

PAOTZU STEAMED BUNS WITH CHICKEN, CABBAGE AND MUSHROOMS

The steamed dumplings could be eaten as part of a Chinese Dim Sum meal.

MAKES about 16

340g/12oz self-raising flour
2 tsps salt
1 tsp fresh yeast
220ml/8 fl oz warm water
120g/4oz cabbage
6 dried black Chinese mushrooms, shiitake
    or cloud ear, pre-soaked
2 tsps sesame oil
225g/8oz minced chicken
1 tbsp chopped fresh root ginger
1 tbsp soy sauce
1 tbsp oyster sauce
Black pepper

1. Place the flour and salt in a large bowl. Sprinkle the yeast on the warm water, stir and leave for 10 minutes, until frothy.

2. Make a well in the centre of the flour, add the liquid and stir in well, gradually incorporating the flour. Cover with a damp cloth and leave in a warm place for 2 hours or until doubled in volume.

3. Finely shred the cabbage and mushrooms. Heat the oil in a wok and add the cabbage, mushrooms and chicken. Stir-fry rapidly for a few minutes. Add the remaining ingredients, stir together and remove from the wok. Leave to cool.

4. Knead the dough for 2-3 minutes, then cut into about 16 pieces. Roll each piece out to a 10cm/4-inch circle and place about 2 tsps of filling on to the centre of each circle.

5. Draw up the edges of the dough, over the filling and pinch together. Place pieces of oiled greaseproof over the pinched ends and turn the buns over to stand on the paper.

6. Leave the buns to stand, covered with the damp cloth, for 15-20 minutes, then place in a steamer and steam rapidly for 10-15 minutes or until firm, springy and well risen. Serve immediately.

TIME: Preparation takes about 40 minutes plus 2 hours 20 minutes for rising. Cooking takes 10-15 minutes.

WATCHPOINT: When steaming the buns, leave enough space between them for them to expand. If necessary, cook in batches.

PREPARATION: Soak the mushrooms for 20 minutes in boiling water. Remove tough stalks before using.

TACOS

Packaged taco shells make this famous Mexican snack easy to prepare, so spend the extra time on imaginative fillings.

MAKES 12

12 taco shells

Chicken Filling

45g/1½oz butter or margarine
1 medium onion, chopped
1 small red pepper, chopped
2 tbsps flaked almonds
340g/12oz chicken breasts, skinned and
    finely chopped
Salt and pepper
1 piece fresh ginger, peeled and chopped
90ml/6 tbsps milk
2 tsps cornflour
140ml/¼ pint sour cream

Toppings

Shredded lettuce
Grated cheese
Tomatoes, seeded and chopped
Chopped spring onions
Avocado slices
Sour cream
Jalapeno peppers
Taco sauce

1. Melt 30g/1oz of the butter or margarine in a medium saucepan and add the onion. Cook slowly until softened.

2. Add the red pepper and almonds and cook slowly until the almonds are lightly browned. Stir often during cooking. Remove to a plate and set aside.

3. Melt the remaining butter in the same saucepan and cook the chicken for about 5 minutes, turning frequently. Season and return the onion mixture to the pan along with the chopped ginger.

4. Blend milk and cornflour and stir into the chicken mixture. Bring to the boil and stir until very thick. Mix in the sour cream and cook gently to heat through. Do not boil.

5. Heat the taco shells on a baking sheet in a preheated 180°C/350°F/Gas Mark 4 oven for 2-3 minutes. Place on the sheet with the open ends down.

6. To fill, hold the shell in one hand and spoon in about 1 tbsp of chicken filling.

7. Next, add a layer of shredded lettuce, followed by a layer of grated cheese. Add your choice of other toppings and finally spoon on some taco sauce.

TIME: Preparation takes about 30 minutes. Cooking takes about 15 minutes for the chicken filling and 2-3 minutes to heat the taco shells.

COOK'S TIP: Placing the taco shells on their open ends when reheating keeps them from closing up and makes filling easier.

SERVING IDEAS: For a buffet, place all the ingredients out separately for guests to help themselves and create their own combinations.

SZECHUAN BANG BANG CHICKEN

Serve this dish as a starter. The diners should toss and mix the ingredients together themselves.

SERVES 4

2 chicken breasts
1 medium cucumber

Sauce
60ml/4 tbsp smooth peanut butter
2 tsp sesame oil
½ tsp sugar
¼ tsp salt
2 tsp stock
½ tsp chilli sauce

1. Simmer the chicken in a pan of water for 30 minutes or until tender. Remove the chicken breasts and cut them into 1.25cm/ ½-inch thick strips.

2. Thinly slice the cucumber. Spread the cucumber on a large serving platter and pile the shredded chicken on top.

3. Mix the peanut butter with the sesame oil, sugar, salt and stock. Pour the sauce evenly over the chicken. Sprinkle the chilli sauce evenly over the top.

TIME: Preparation takes about 15 minutes and cooking takes 30 minutes.

VARIATION: Use crunchy peanut butter or tahini in place of smooth peanut butter.

PREPARATION: The chicken is cooked when the juices run clear as a sharp knife or skewer is inserted into the thickest part of the meat.

CHICKEN ESCALOPES

There are a multitude of different methods of cooking chicken, and this one although one of the simplest, is also one of the most delicious.

SERVES 4

4 chicken breasts, boned and skinned
1 egg
30g/8 tbsps wholemeal breadcrumbs
1 tbsp chopped fresh sage
Salt and freshly ground black pepper
2 tbsps walnut oil
120ml/4 fl oz mayonnaise
140ml/¼ pint natural unset yogurt
1 tsp grated fresh horseradish
2 tbsps chopped walnuts
Lemon slices and chopped walnuts to
    garnish

1. Pat the chicken breasts dry with kitchen paper.
2. Whisk the egg with a fork until it just begins to froth.
3. Carefully brush all surfaces of the chicken breasts with the egg.

4. Put the breadcrumbs onto a shallow plate and mix in the chopped sage. Season with a little salt and freshly ground black pepper.
5. Place the chicken breasts, one at a time, onto the plate and carefully press the crumb mixture onto the surfaces of the chicken.
6. Put the oil into a large shallow pan, and gently fry the prepared chicken breasts on each side for 6-7 minutes until they are lightly golden and tender. Set them aside, and keep warm.
7. Mix all the remaining ingredients except for the garnish, in a small bowl, whisking well to blend the yogurt and mayonnaise evenly.
8. Place the cooked chicken breasts on a serving dish, and spoon a little of the sauce over. Serve garnished with the lemon slices and additional chopped nuts.

TIME: Preparation takes about 20 minutes, cooking takes about 15 minutes.

VARIATIONS: Use almonds instead of walnuts in this recipe, and limes instead of lemons. Oranges and hazelnuts make another delicious variation.

SERVING IDEAS: Serve with lightly cooked French beans and new potatoes, or rice.

SALADE BRESSE

As well as being famous for its cheese Bresse, in Burgundy, is renowned for its special breed of chickens, reputed to be the best in France.

SERVES 4-6

1 head radicchio, leaves separated and washed
1 head cos lettuce, washed
1 bunch lamb's lettuce or watercress, washed
4 chicken breasts, cooked, skinned and thinly sliced
120g/4oz Bresse Bleu or other blue cheese, cut in small pieces
16 cornichons (small pickled gherkins) thinly sliced
120g/4oz cherry tomatoes, halved and cored
60g/2oz walnut halves

Dressing
2 tbsps vegetable and walnut oil mixed
2 tsps white wine vinegar
175ml/6 fl oz crème frâiche
2 tsps chopped fresh tarragon
Salt and pepper

1. Tear the radicchio and cos lettuce into bite-size pieces. Leave the lamb's lettuce in whole leaves. If using watercress, wash thoroughly, remove the thick stems and yellow leaves.

2. Toss the lettuces together and pile onto a salad plate.

3. Place the chicken, cheese, cornichons, tomatoes and walnuts on top of the lettuce.

4. Mix the oils and vinegar together and whisk well to emulsify.

5. Fold in the crème frâiche and add the tarragon, salt and pepper.

6. Drizzle some of the dressing over the salad to serve.

TIME: Preparation takes about 20 minutes.

VARIATION: Use Gorgonzola instead of Bresse Bleu, and yogurt or soured cream in place of the crème frâiche.

PREPARATION: The dressing can be made in advance and kept refrigerated.

CHICKEN WITH BLACKCURRANT SAUCE

The sharp tang of blackcurrants makes an ideal partner for chicken.

SERVES 4

4 chicken breasts, boned and skinned
3 tbsps sesame oil
225g/8oz fresh blackcurrants
Juice of 1 orange
140ml/¼ pint red wine
Sugar to taste
Orange slices and fresh blackcurrants to
    garnish

1. Season the chicken breasts with a little salt. Heat the oil in a frying pan.

2. Gently sauté the chicken breasts for 6-7 minutes on each side, until they are golden brown and tender.

3. Meanwhile put the blackcurrants in a small pan, along with the orange juice and red wine. Bring to the boil, then cover and simmer gently until the blackcurrants are soft.

4. Using a liquidiser or food processor, blend the blackcurrants and the cooking juice for 30 seconds.

5. Rub the blended purée through a fine nylon sieve using the back of a wooden spoon, pressing the fruit through to reserve all the juice and pulp but leaving the pips in the sieve.

6. Put the sieved purée into a small saucepan and heat gently, stirring constantly until the liquid has reduced and the sauce is thick and smooth. Add a little sugar if the sauce is too sour.

7. Arrange the chicken breasts on a serving dish, and spoon the blackcurrant sauce over. Garnish with orange slices and fresh blackcurrants.

TIME: Preparation takes 15 minutes, cooking takes approximately 15 minutes.

PREPARATION: To test if the chicken breasts are cooked, insert a skewer into the thickest part, then press gently, if the juices run clear, the meat is cooked.

VARIATION: Use blackberries instead of blackcurrants in this recipe.

PEKING EGG BATTERED CHICKEN WITH BEAN SPROUTS, IN ONION AND GARLIC SAUCE

This exciting mixture results in a simply delicious dish.

SERVES 3

3 chicken breasts
Salt and pepper
2 eggs
2 cloves garlic
2 spring onions
60ml/4 tbsps oil
175g/6oz fresh bean sprouts
60ml/4 tbsps stock
Vinegar to taste

1. Cut each chicken breast crosswise into 2.5cm/1-inch slices. Rub with salt and pepper.

2. Beat eggs lightly, and add the chicken slices to the eggs.

3. Crush the garlic and cut spring onions into 2.5cm/1-inch pieces.

4. Heat the oil in the wok. Add the chicken pieces one by one, and reduce heat to low. Leave to sauté for 2-3 minutes.

5. Once the egg has set, sprinkle the chicken with garlic, spring onion and bean sprouts.

6. Finally, add the stock and vinegar to taste. Simmer gently for 4 minutes.

7. Remove the chicken, cut each piece into small regular pieces, serve on a heated platter. Pour the remaining sauce from the pan over the chicken.

TIME: Preparation takes 10 minutes, cooking takes about 10 minutes.

COOK'S TIP: Buy the bean sprouts on the day you intend to use them as they deteriorate rapidly.

SERVING IDEAS: Serve with a chilli dipping sauce and rice.

CHICKEN WITH WALNUTS & CELERY

Oyster sauce lends a subtle, slightly salty taste to this Cantonese dish.

SERVES 4

225g/8oz boned chicken, cut into 2.5cm/
    1-inch pieces
2 tsps soy sauce
2 tsps brandy
1 tsp cornflour
Salt and pepper
2 tbsps oil
1 clove garlic
120g/4oz walnut halves
3 sticks celery, cut in diagonal slices
140ml/¼ pint chicken stock
2 tsps oyster sauce

1. Combine the chicken with the soy sauce, brandy, cornflour, salt and pepper.

2. Heat a wok and add the oil and garlic. Cook for about 1 minute to flavour the oil.

3. Remove the garlic and add the chicken in two batches. Stir-fry quickly to cook the chicken but without allowing it to brown. Remove the chicken and add the walnuts to the wok. Cook for about 2 minutes until the walnuts are slightly brown and crisp.

4. Add the celery to the wok and cook for about 1 minute. Add the stock and oyster sauce and bring to the boil. When boiling, return the chicken to the pan and stir to coat all the ingredients well. Serve immediately.

TIME: Preparation takes about 20 minutes, cooking takes about 8 minutes.

WATCHPOINT: Nuts can burn very easily. Stir them constantly for even browning.

VARIATION: Almonds or cashew nuts may be used instead of the walnuts. If the cashew nuts are already roasted, add them along with the celery.

FLAUTAS

Traditionally, these are long, thin rolls of tortillas with savoury fillings,
topped with sour cream.

SERVES 6

225g/8oz chicken, skinned, boned and
    minced or finely chopped
1 tbsp oil
1 small onion, finely chopped
½ green pepper, finely chopped
½-1 chilli, seeded and finely chopped
90g/3oz frozen sweetcorn
6 black olives, pitted and chopped
120ml/4 fl oz double cream
Salt
12 tortillas
Taco sauce, guacamole and sour cream for
    toppings

1. Use a food processor or meat mincer to prepare the chicken, or chop by hand.

2. Heat the oil in a medium frying pan and add the chicken, onion and green pepper. Cook over a moderate heat, stirring frequently to break up the pieces of chicken.

3. When the chicken is cooked and the vegetables are softened, add the chilli, sweetcorn, olives, cream and salt. Bring to the boil over a high heat and boil rapidly, stirring continuously, to reduce and thicken the cream.

4. Place 2 tortillas on a clean work surface, overlapping them by about 5cm/2 inches. Spoon some of the chicken mixture onto the tortillas, roll up and secure with cocktail sticks.

5. Fry the flautas in about 1.25cm/½ inch oil in a large frying pan. Do not allow the tortillas to get very brown. Drain on kitchen paper.

6. Arrange flautas on serving plates and top with sour cream, guacamole and taco sauce.

TIME: Preparation takes about 15 minutes and cooking takes about
15 minutes.

BUYING GUIDE: Prepared tortillas can be bought from large supermarkets.

SERVING IDEAS: Flautas are often served with rice, refried beans and a
salad.

AUBERGINE AND CHICKEN CHILLI

This unusual dish is both delicious and filling.

SERVES 4

2 medium-sized aubergines
60ml/4 tbsps sesame oil
2 cloves garlic, crushed
4 spring onions thinly sliced, diagonally
1 green chilli, finely chopped
340g/12oz boned and skinned chicken
    breast
60ml/4 tbsps light soy sauce
2 tbsps stock, or water
1 tbsp tomato purée
1 tsp cornflour
Sugar to taste

1. Cut the aubergines into quarters lengthways, using a sharp knife. Slice the aubergine quarters into pieces approximately 1.25cm/½-inch thick.

2. Put the aubergine slices into a bowl and sprinkle liberally with salt. Stir well to coat evenly. Cover with cling film and leave to stand for 30 minutes.

3. Rinse the aubergine slices very thoroughly under running water, then pat dry.

4. Heat half of the oil in a wok, or large frying pan, and gently cook the garlic until it is soft, but not coloured.

5. Add the aubergine slices to the wok and cook, stirring frequently, for 3-4 minutes.

6. Stir the spring onions together with the chilli into the cooked aubergine, and cook for a further 1 minute. Remove from the pan, and set aside, keeping warm.

7. Cut the chicken breast into thin slices with a sharp knife.

8. Heat the remaining 2 tbsps of oil in the wok, and fry the chicken pieces for approximately 2 minutes or until they have turned white and are thoroughly cooked.

9. Return the aubergine and spring onions to the pan and cook, stirring continuously, for 2 minutes or until heated through completely.

10. Mix together the remaining ingredients and pour these over the chicken and aubergines in the wok, stirring constantly until the sauce has thickened and cleared. Serve immediately.

TIME: Preparation takes about 10 minutes plus 30 minutes marinating, cooking takes approximately 15 minutes.

COOK'S TIP: The vegetables can be prepared well in advance, but the aubergines should be removed from the salt after 30 minutes, or they will become too dehydrated.

VARIATION: Use courgettes in place of the aubergines if wished.

CHICKEN WITH CLOUD EARS

Cloud ears is the delightful name for an edible tree fungus which is mushroom-like in taste and texture.

SERVES 6

12 cloud ears, wood ears or other dried
    Chinese mushrooms, soaked in boiling
    water for 5 minutes
450g/1lb chicken breasts, boned and thinly
    sliced crosswise
1 egg white
2 tsps cornflour
2 tsps white wine
2 tsps sesame oil
280ml/½ pint oil
2.5cm/1-inch piece fresh root ginger
1 clove garlic
280ml/½ pint chicken stock
1 tbsp cornflour
3 tbsps light soy sauce
Pinch salt and pepper

1. Soak the mushrooms until they soften and swell. Remove all the skin and bone from the chicken and cut it into thin slices. Mix the chicken with the egg white, cornflour, wine and sesame oil.

2. Heat the wok for a few minutes and pour in the oil. Add the whole piece of ginger and whole garlic clove to the oil and cook for about 1 minute. Take them out and reduce the heat.

3. Add about a quarter of the chicken at a time and stir-fry for about 1 minute. Remove and continue cooking until all the chicken is fried. Remove all but about 2 tbsps of the oil from the wok.

4. Drain the mushrooms and squeeze them to extract all the liquid. If using mushrooms with stems, remove the stems before slicing the caps thinly. Cut cloud ears or wood ears into smaller pieces. Add to the wok and cook for about 1 minute.

5. Add the stock and allow it to come almost to the boil. Mix together the cornflour and soy sauce and add a spoonful of the hot stock. Add the mixture to the wok, stirring constantly, and bring to the boil. Allow to boil for 1-2 minutes or until thickened. The sauce will clear when the cornflour has cooked sufficiently.

6. Return the chicken to the wok and add salt and pepper. Stir thoroughly for about 1 minute and serve immediately.

TIME: Preparation takes about 25 minutes, cooking takes about 5 minutes.

VARIATION: Flat, cup or button mushrooms may be used instead of the dried mushrooms. Eliminate the soaking and slice them thickly. Cook as for the dried variety. Two tsps bottled oyster sauce may be added with the stock.

BUYING GUIDE: Cloud ears or wood ears are both available from Chinese supermarkets and some delicatessens. Chinese shiitake mushrooms are more readily available fresh or dried. Both keep a long time in their dried state.

CHICKEN, HAM AND LEEK PIE

The addition of cream and egg yolks at the end of the cooking time makes this pie extra special.

SERVES 6-8

1 × 1.5kg/3lb chicken
1 onion
1 bay leaf
Parsley stalks
Salt and black pepper
450g/1lb leeks
30g/1oz butter
120g/4oz cooked ham, chopped
1 tbsp parsley
280ml/½ pint chicken stock
340-400g/12-14oz puff pastry
140ml/¼ pint double cream
1 egg, lightly beaten for glazing

1. Put the cleaned chicken in a large saucepan together with the onion, bay leaf, parsley stalks and salt and pepper. Cover with cold water and bring gently to the boil. Allow to simmer for about 45 minutes until the chicken is tender. Leave it to cool in the pan.

2. Meanwhile, wash and trim the leeks and cut into 3.75cm/1½-inch pieces. Melt the butter in a small pan and gently sauté the leeks for about 5 minutes. Remove from the heat.

3. Take the cooled chicken out of the pan, remove the skin and strip off the flesh. Cut it into good-sized pieces.

4. Put the chicken, ham, leeks and parsley into a large pie dish with plenty of seasoning. Pour over 280ml/½ pint of the stock from the chicken.

5. Roll out the pastry slightly larger than the size of the pie dish. Use the trimmings to line the rim of the dish. Dampen them and put on the pastry lid. Trim and seal the edges together firmly. Any surplus pastry can be used to make decorative leaves. Cut a few slits in the pastry to allow the steam to escape. Brush the pastry well with beaten egg.

6. Bake in the centre of a preheated 230°C/450°F/Gas Mark 8 oven for 15 minutes, remove and glaze again with beaten egg. Reduce the temperature of the oven to 200°C/400°F/Gas Mark 6. Return the pie to the oven for another 20 minutes.

7. When the pie crust is well risen and golden brown, remove it from the oven and carefully lift off a segment of pastry and pour in the cream which has been gently warmed together with the remaining beaten egg.

TIME: Preparation takes about 45 minutes for the chicken plus extra cooling time and 20 minutes to prepare the pie. Cooking takes about 35 minutes.

SERVING IDEAS: Serve with creamed potatoes and a green vegetable.

CRUMB FRIED CHICKEN

*A southern speciality, this dish has a slightly misleading name since
most of the 'frying' is done in the oven!*

SERVES 4-6

1.5kg/3lb chicken
120g/4oz breadcrumbs
60g/2oz Parmesan cheese
¼ tsp ground ginger
2 eggs, mixed with a pinch of salt
3 tbsps oil
60g/2oz butter or margarine
Lemons and parsley for garnish

---

1. Preheat the oven to 200°C/400°F/Gas Mark 6. To joint the chicken, first cut off the legs, bending them outwards to break the ball and socket joint. Cut in between the ball and socket joint to completely remove the legs.

2. Cut down the breastbone with sharp poultry shears to separate the two halves. Use the poultry shears to cut through the rib cage. Use the notch in the shears to separate the wing joints from the back.

3. Use a sharp knife to separate the drumstick from the thigh. Cut the breasts in half with poultry shears.

4. Mix the breadcrumbs, Parmesan cheese and ground ginger together. First dip the chicken into the egg and then coat with the crumbs.

5. Heat the oil in a large frying pan and add the butter. When hot, place in the chicken, skin side down first. Cook both sides until golden brown.

6. Transfer with a slotted spoon to a baking sheet and place in the oven for 20-30 minutes, or until the juices run clear when the chicken is tested with a knife or a fork. Serve garnished with small bunches of parsley and lemon wedges or slices.

TIME: Preparation takes about 30 minutes. If using pre-jointed chicken, allow about 15-20 minutes for preparation. Chicken will take about 10-15 minutes to brown and 20-30 minutes to finish cooking in the oven.

PREPARATION: Mix the crumbs, cheese and ginger on a sheet of greaseproof paper. Place the chicken on the crumbs and shake the paper from side to side to coat easily and completely.

VARIATIONS: If wished, leave out the Parmesan cheese and ginger and add extra breadcrumbs, paprika, salt, pepper and a pinch of thyme.

INDIAN CHICKEN

Marinating chicken with spices allows their full flavours to penetrate the meat.

SERVES 4-6

1 × 1.5kg/3lb chicken, cut into 8 pieces
570ml/1 pint natural yogurt
2 tsps ground coriander
2 tsps paprika
1 tsp ground turmeric
Juice of 1 lime
1 tbsp honey
½ clove garlic, crushed
1 small piece ginger, peeled and grated

1. Pierce the chicken all over with a fork or skewer.

2. Combine all the remaining ingredients and spread half the mixture over the chicken, rubbing in well.

3. Place the chicken in a shallow dish or a plastic bag and cover or tie and leave for at least 4 hours or overnight in the refrigerator.

4. Arrange the chicken skin side down under a moderate pre-heated grill and cook until lightly browned, turn over and cook the second side until lightly browned, this should take about 30 minutes in all. Baste frequently with remaining marinade.

5. Lower the grill and cook for 15 minutes, turning and basting frequently, until the chicken is brown and the skin is crisp.

6. Alternatively, cook the chicken in a covered pan in the oven at 180°C/325°F/Gas Mark 4 for 45 minutes - 1 hour and grill for the last 15 minutes for flavour and colour.

7. Serve any remaining yogurt mixture separately as a sauce.

TIME: Preparation takes about 15 minutes and marinating at least 4 hours, cooking takes about 45 minutes.

COOK'S TIP: If you wish, the chicken can be barbecued, but make sure the shelf is on the level furthest from the coals so that the chicken has time to cook without burning.

VARIATION: Use chicken breasts only for this dish.

CHICKEN LIVERS WITH PEPPERS

Chicken livers are often overlooked as a tasty and nutritious food.

SERVES 4

4 dried Chinese shiitake mushrooms
450g/1lb chicken livers
30g/1oz fresh root ginger
1 tbsp rice vinegar
2 tsps sugar
1 small leek
1 onion
1 green pepper
1 red pepper
3 tbsps vegetable oil
2 spring onion 'brushes' to garnish

1. Soak mushrooms in hot water for 20 minutes.

2. Clean and trim chicken livers, and blanch in boiling water for 3 minutes. Drain and slice.

3. Peel and finely slice ginger. Mix the vinegar and sugar, add the ginger and set aside.

4. Clean and trim the leek and cut into thin rings. Peel and slice the onion and cut into strips. Core and remove seeds from peppers, and cut into strips.

5. Drain the mushrooms, remove hard stalks, and cut caps into thin slices.

6. Heat a wok, add the oil, and, when hot, add the mushrooms, onion, leek and peppers, and stir-fry for 5 minutes. Remove and set aside.

7. Add the liver and the ginger mixture. Stir-fry for a further 5 minutes, return vegetable mixture to wok and heat through. Serve garnished with spring onion 'brushes'.

TIME: Preparation takes 25 minutes and cooking takes about 15 minutes.

PREPARATION: To make spring onion 'brushes', trim and slice the onion lengthwise, keeping the root end intact. Put into iced water and refrigerate until curled.

BUYING GUIDE: Dried shiitake mushrooms are available from Oriental stores. Some large supermarkets now sell fresh shiitake mushrooms, which don't require any soaking.

CHICKEN AND VEGETABLE STEW

A combination of chicken, broad beans, peppers and onions made into an aromatic stew.

SERVES 4-6

1 × 1.5kg/3lb chicken, cut in 8 pieces
90g/3oz butter or margarine
3 tbsps flour
1 large red pepper, diced
1 large green pepper, diced
6 spring onions, chopped
430ml/¾ pint chicken stock
180g/6oz broad beans
1 tsp chopped thyme
Salt, pepper and pinch nutmeg

1. To cut the chicken in 8 pieces, remove the legs first. Cut between the legs and the body of the chicken.

2. Bend the legs outwards to break the joint and cut away from the body.

3. Cut the drumstick and thigh joints in half.

4. Cut down the breastbone with a sharp knife and then use poultry shears to cut through the bone and ribcage to remove the breast joints from the back.

5. Cut both breast joints in half, leaving some white meat attached to the wing joint.

6. Heat the butter in a large frying pan and when foaming add the chicken, skin side down. Brown on one side, turn over and brown other side. Remove the chicken and add the flour to the pan. Cook to a pale straw colour. Add the peppers and onions and cook briefly.

7. Gradually stir in the chicken stock and bring to the boil. Stir constantly until thickened. Add the chicken, broad beans, thyme, seasoning and nutmeg. Cover the pan and cook about 25 minutes, or until the chicken is tender.

TIME: Preparation takes about 35 minutes and cooking takes about 40 minutes.

PREPARATION: For crisper vegetables, add them after the chicken and sauce have cooked for about 15 minutes.

BUYING GUIDE: Buying a whole chicken and jointing it yourself is cheaper than buying chicken joints.

CHICKEN WITH SAFFRON RICE AND PEAS

Saffron is frequently used in Spanish recipes. While it is expensive, it gives rice and sauces a lovely golden colour and delicate taste.

SERVES 4

2 tbsps oil
1 × 900g-1.5kg/2-3lb chicken, cut into 8
    pieces and skinned if wished
Salt and pepper
1 small onion, finely chopped
2 tsps paprika
1 clove garlic, crushed
8 tomatoes, skinned, seeded and chopped
300g/10oz rice
700ml/1¼ pints boiling water
Large pinch saffron or 1.25ml/¼ tsp ground
    saffron
175g/6oz frozen peas
2 tbsps chopped parsley

1. Heat the oil in a large frying pan. Season the chicken with salt and pepper and place it in the hot oil, skin side down first. Cook over moderate heat, turning the chicken frequently to brown it lightly. Set the chicken aside.

2. Add the onions to the oil and cook slowly until softened but not coloured.

3. Add the paprika and cook for about 2 minutes, stirring frequently until the paprika loses some of its red colour. Add the garlic and the tomatoes.

4. Cook the mixture over high heat for about 5 minutes to evaporate the liquid from the tomatoes. The mixture should be of dropping consistency when done. Add the rice, water and saffron and stir together.

5. Return the chicken to the casserole and bring to the boil over high heat. Reduce to simmering, cover tightly and cook for about 20 minutes. Remove chicken and add the peas and parsley. Cook a further 5-10 minutes, or until rice is tender. Combine with the chicken to serve.

TIME: Preparation takes about 20-25 minutes and cooking takes about 25-35 minutes.

VARIATION: If using fresh peas, allow about 400g/14oz of peas in their pods. Cook fresh peas with the rice and chicken.

SERVING IDEAS: This is a very casual, peasant-type dish which is traditionally served in the casserole in which it was cooked.

STIR-FRIED MINCED CHICKEN ON CRISPY NOODLES

Deep-fried crispy noodles are teamed up with the distinctively Oriental flavour of ginger and chicken in this simple recipe.

SERVES 2-3

225g/½lb chicken breast meat
2 slices cooked smoked ham
6 slices fresh root ginger
1 large onion
3 spring onions
3 tbsps oil
½ tsp salt
2 tbsps soy sauce
2 tbsps chicken stock
1 tbsp vinegar
1 tsp chilli sauce
1 tsp sugar
2 tsp cornflour

Crispy Noodles
450g/1lb egg noodles
Oil for deep frying
Salt
Sesame seed oil

1. Cook the noodles in boiling, salted water for 12-14 minutes, stirring occasionally.

2. Meanwhile, mince the chicken. Finely shred the ham, ginger and onion. Slice the spring onions.

3. Heat the oil in a large frying pan and add the onion, ham and ginger. Stir-fry for 2 minutes.

4. Add the minced chicken. Sprinkle with the salt, soy sauce and stock. Stir-fry for a further 5 minutes.

5. Add the vinegar, sherry, chilli sauce, sugar, spring onions, and cornflour blended with 2 tbsps water. Cook over high heat for 2 minutes.

6. When the noodles are cooked, drain well and pat dry with absorbent paper.

7. Fry the noodles in hot oil for 2-3 minutes until very crisp. Drain well and sprinkle with salt and sesame seed oil.

8. Serve the chicken on a heated platter with the crispy noodles.

TIME: Preparation takes about 20 minutes, cooking takes about 10 minutes for the chicken and 12-14 for the noodles.

COOK'S TIP: Chilli sauce can be found alongside the soy sauce in most good supermarkets.

CHICKEN COBBLER

This dish is warming winter fare with its creamy sauce and tender, light topping.

SERVES 6

4 chicken joints: 2 breasts and 2 legs
1.5 litres/2½ pints water
1 bay leaf
4 whole peppercorns
2 carrots, peeled and diced
24 button onions, peeled
90g/6 tbsps frozen sweetcorn
140ml/¼ pint double cream
Salt

Cobbler Topping
400g/14oz plain flour
1½ tbsps baking powder
Pinch salt
75g/2½oz butter or margarine
340ml/12 fl oz milk
1 egg, beaten with a pinch of salt

1. Place the chicken in a deep saucepan with the water, bay leaf and peppercorns. Cover and bring to the boil. Reduce the heat and allow to simmer for 20-30 minutes, or until the chicken is tender. Remove the chicken from the pan and allow to cool. Skim and discard the fat from the surface of the stock.

2. Continue to simmer the stock until reduced by about half. Meanwhile, skin the chicken and remove the meat from the bones. Strain the stock and add the carrots and onions. Cook until tender and add the sweetcorn. Stir in the cream, season and add the chicken. Pour into a warmed casserole or into individual baking dishes and keep hot.

3. To prepare the topping, sift the dry ingredients into a bowl or place them in a food processor and process once or twice to sift.

4. Rub in the butter or margarine until the mixture resembles breadcrumbs. Stir in enough of the milk until the mixture comes together. If using a food processor trickle the milk in down the food tube and process in short bursts to avoid overmixing.

5. Turn out onto a floured surface and knead lightly. Roll out with a floured rolling pin until it is about 1.25cm/½-inch thick.

6. Cut the dough into rounds using a 5cm/2-inch cutter to form the cobbles. Place the rounds on top of the chicken mixture and brush the surface of the cobbler with the egg and salt mixture and bake for 10-15 minutes in a pre-heated oven at 190°C/375°F/Gas Mark 5. Serve immediately.

TIME: Preparation takes about 20-30 minutes for the chicken, about 20 minutes to prepare the sauce, and the cobbler takes about 10 minutes to prepare. Final cooking takes about 10-15 minutes.

PREPARATION: Once the topping has been prepared it must be baked immediately or the baking powder will stop working and the cobbler topping will not rise.

SESAME FRIED CHICKEN

Sesame seeds add a lovely nutty flavour to chicken.

SERVES 4

120g/4oz plain flour
1 tsp salt
1 tsp pepper
2 tsps paprika
60g/2oz sesame seeds
450g/1lb chicken breasts, or 4 good-sized
    pieces
1 egg, beaten, with 1 tbsp water
3 tbsps olive oil

1. Sift flour onto a sheet of greaseproof paper and stir in salt, pepper, paprika and sesame seeds.

2. Dip chicken breasts in the egg and water mixture, then coat well in seasoned flour.

3. Heat a wok or frying pan, add oil and, when hot, fry the chicken breasts until golden brown on both sides.

4. Turn heat down, and cook gently for 10 minutes on each side.

TIME: Preparation takes 10 minutes and cooking takes about 25 minutes.

PREPARATION: Add a little cayenne pepper to the paprika to make a spicy coating.

SERVING IDEAS: Serve with rice or new potatoes and carrots.

LEMON CHICKEN

Chicken, lemon and basil is an ideal flavour combination and one that is used often in Greek cookery.

SERVES 4-6

2 tbsps olive oil
30g/1oz butter or margarine
1 × 1.5kg/3lb chicken, jointed
1 small onion, cut in thin strips
2 sticks celery, shredded
2 carrots, cut in julienne strips
1 tbsp chopped fresh basil
1 bay leaf
Grated rind and juice of 2 small lemons
140ml/¼ pint water
Salt and pepper
Pinch sugar (optional)
Lemon slices for garnishing

1. Heat the oil in a large frying pan. Add the butter or margarine and, when foaming, place in the chicken, skin side down, in one layer. Brown and turn over. Brown the other side. Cook the chicken in two batches if necessary. Remove the chicken to a plate and set aside.

2. Add the vegetables and cook for 2-3 minutes over a moderate heat. Add the basil, bay leaf, lemon rind and juice, water, salt and pepper and replace the chicken. Bring the mixture to the boil.

3. Cover the pan and reduce the heat. Allow to simmer about 35-45 minutes or until the chicken is tender and the juices run clear when the thighs are pierced with a fork.

4. Remove the chicken and vegetables to a serving dish and discard the bay leaf. The sauce should be thick, so boil to reduce if necessary. If the sauce is too tart, add a pinch of sugar. Spoon the sauce over the chicken to serve and garnish with the lemon slices.

TIME: Preparation takes about 30 minutes, cooking takes about 45-55 minutes total, including browning of chicken.

VARIATIONS: Use limes instead of lemons and oregano instead of basil.

SERVING IDEAS: In Greece, this dish is often served with pasta. Rice is also a good accompaniment, along with a green salad.

TOMATO AND BACON FRIED CHICKEN

Not the usual crisp fried chicken, this is cooked in a tomato sauce flavoured with garlic, herbs and wine.

SERVES 6

Flour for dredging
Salt and pepper
1 × 1.5kg/3lb chicken, cut into portions
90ml/6 tbsps oil
75g/2½oz butter or margarine
1 clove garlic, crushed
1 small onion, finely chopped
120g/4oz streaky bacon, diced
6 tomatoes, skinned and chopped
2 tsps fresh thyme or 1 tsp dried thyme
Salt and pepper
140ml/¼ pint white wine
2 tbsps chopped parsley

1. Mix the flour with salt and pepper and dredge the chicken lightly, shaking the pieces to remove any excess flour. Heat the oil in a large frying pan and, when hot, add the butter.

2. Add the chicken drumstick and thigh pieces skin side down and allow to brown. Turn the pieces over and brown on the other side. Brown over moderately low heat so that the chicken cooks as well as browns. Push the chicken to one side of the pan, add the breast meat, and brown in the same way.

3. Add the garlic, onion and bacon to the pan and lower the heat. Cook slowly for about 10 minutes, or until the bacon browns slightly. Add the tomatoes and thyme and lower the heat. Cook until the chicken is just tender and the tomatoes are softened.

4. Using a draining spoon, transfer the chicken and other ingredients to a serving dish and keep warm. Remove all but about 60ml/4 tbsps of the fat from the pan and deglaze with the wine, scraping up the browned bits from the bottom. Bring to the boil and allow to reduce slightly. Pour over the chicken to serve, and sprinkle with chopped parsley.

TIME: Preparation takes about 25 minutes and cooking takes about 30-40 minutes.

PREPARATION: Brown the chicken slowly so that it cooks at the same time as it browns. This will cut down on the length of cooking time needed once all the ingredients are added.

SPICY SPANISH CHICKEN

*Chilli, coriander and sunny tomatoes add warm Spanish flavour
to grilled chicken.*

SERVES 6

6 boned chicken breasts

Grated rind and juice of 1 lime

2 tbsps olive oil

Coarsely ground black pepper

90ml/6 tbsps whole grain mustard

2 tsps paprika

4 ripe tomatoes, skinned, seeded and
  quartered

2 shallots, chopped

1 clove garlic, crushed

½ Jalapeno pepper or other chilli, seeded
  and chopped

1 tsp wine vinegar

Pinch salt

2 tbsps chopped fresh coriander

Whole coriander leaves to garnish

1. Place the chicken breasts in a shallow dish with the lime rind and juice, oil, pepper, mustard and paprika. Marinate for about 1 hour, turning occasionally.

2. To skin the tomatoes easily, drop them into boiling water for about 5 seconds or less depending on ripeness. Place immediately in cold water. Skins should come off easily.

3. Place the tomatoes, shallots, garlic, chilli, vinegar and salt in a food processor or blender and process until coarsely chopped. Stir in the coriander by hand.

4. Place the chicken on a grill pan and reserve the marinade. Cook the chicken skin side uppermost for about 7-10 minutes, depending on how close the chicken is to the heat source. Baste frequently with the remaining marinade. Grill the other side in the same way. Sprinkle with salt after grilling.

5. Place the chicken on serving plates and garnish the top with coriander leaves or sprigs. Serve with a spoonful of the tomato relish on one side.

TIME: Preparation takes about 1 hour including marinating, and cooking takes 14-20 minutes.

PREPARATION: Tomato relish can be prepared in advance and kept in the refrigerator.

WATCHPOINT: When preparing chillies, wear rubber gloves or at least be sure to wash hands thoroughly after handling them. Do not touch eyes or face before washing hands.

CHICKEN POLISH STYLE

Choose small, young chickens for a truly Polish style dish. A dried white roll was originally used for stuffing, but breadcrumbs are easier.

SERVES 4

2 × 900g/2lb chickens
15g/½oz butter or margarine
2 chicken livers
6 slices bread, made into crumbs
2 tsps chopped parsley
1 tsp chopped dill
1 egg
Salt and pepper
140ml/¼ pint chicken stock

1. Remove the fat from just inside the cavities of the chickens and discard it. Melt the butter in a small frying pan. Pick over the chicken livers and cut away any discoloured portions. Add chicken livers to the butter and cook until just brown. Chop and set aside.

2. Combine the breadcrumbs, herbs, egg, salt and pepper and mix well. Mix in the chopped chicken livers.

3. Stuff the cavities of the chickens and sew up the openings. Tie the legs together.

4. Place the chickens in a roasting tin and spread the breasts and legs lightly with more butter. Pour the stock around the chickens and roast in a preheated 190°C/375°F/Gas Mark 5 oven for about 40-45 minutes. Baste frequently with the pan juices during roasting.

5. To check if the chickens are done, pierce the thickest part of the thigh with a skewer or small, sharp knife. If the juices run clear the chickens are ready. If the juices are pink, return to the oven for another 5-10 minutes.

6. When the chickens are done, remove them from the roasting pan, remove the string and keep them warm. Skim any fat from the surface of the pan juices. If a lot of liquid has accumulated, pour into a small saucepan and reduce over high heat. Pour the juices over the chicken to serve.

TIME: Preparation takes about 20 minutes and cooking takes about 45 minutes.

SERVING IDEAS: Serve with a cucumber salad or a Polish style lettuce salad and new potatoes tossed with butter and dill.

VARIATIONS: Chopped mushrooms or onions may be added to the stuffing, if wished.

CHICKEN, SAUSAGE AND OKRA STEW

There is an exotic taste to this economical chicken stew. The garlic sausage adds flavour instantly.

SERVES 4-6

120ml/4 fl oz oil
1 × 1.5kg/3lb chicken, cut into 6-8 pieces
120g/4oz flour
1 large onion, finely chopped
1 large green pepper, roughly chopped
3 sticks celery, finely chopped
2 cloves garlic, crushed
225g/8oz garlic sausage, diced
1150ml/2 pints chicken stock
1 bay leaf
Dash tabasco
Salt and pepper
120g/4oz fresh okra
Cooked rice to serve

1. Heat the oil in a large frying pan and brown the chicken on both sides, 3-4 pieces at a time. Transfer the chicken to a plate and set it aside.

2. Lower the heat under the pan and add the flour. Cook over a very low heat for about 30 minutes, stirring constantly until the flour turns a rich, dark brown. Take the pan off the heat occasionally, so that the flour does not burn.

3. Add the onion, green pepper, celery, garlic and sausage to the pan and cook for about 5 minutes over very low heat, stirring continuously.

4. Slowly add the stock, stirring constantly, and bring to the boil. Add the bay leaf, a dash of tabasco and seasoning. Return the chicken to the pan, cover and cook for about 30 minutes or until the chicken is tender.

5. Top and tail the okra and cut each part into 2-3 pieces. If okra are small, leave whole. Add to the chicken and cook for a further 10-15 minutes. Remove the bay leaf and serve over rice.

TIME: Preparation takes about 30 minutes and cooking takes about 1 hour 25 minutes.

COOK'S TIP: The oil and flour roux may be made ahead of time and kept in the refrigerator to use whenever needed. If the roux is cold, heat the liquid before adding.

FRIED CHICKEN

Fried Chicken is easy to make at home and it's much better than a take away!

SERVES 4

2 eggs
1.5kg/3lb chicken portions
225g/8oz flour
1 tsp each salt, paprika and sage
½ tsp black pepper
Pinch cayenne pepper (optional)
Oil for frying
Parsley or watercress to garnish

1. Beat the eggs in a large bowl and add the chicken one piece at a time, turning to coat.

2. Mix flour and seasonings in a large plastic bag.

3. Place the chicken into the bag one piece at a time, close bag tightly and shake to coat. Alternatively, dip each chicken piece in a bowl of seasoned flour, shaking off the excess.

4. Heat about 1.25cm/½ inch of oil in a large frying pan.

5. When the oil is hot, add the chicken skin side down first. Fry for about 12 minutes and then turn over. Fry a further 12 minutes or until the juices run clear.

6. Drain the chicken on kitchen paper and serve immediately. Garnish with parsley or watercress.

TIME: Preparation takes about 20 minutes and cooking takes about 24 minutes.

PREPARATION: The chicken should not be crowded in the frying pan. If the pan is small, fry the chicken in several batches.

COOK'S TIP: When coating anything for frying, be sure to coat it just before cooking. If left to stand, the coating will usually become very soggy.

TANGERINE PEEL CHICKEN

An exotic mixture of flavours blend perfectly in this delicious chicken dish.

SERVES 2

450g/1lb boned chicken breast, cut into 2.5cm/1-inch pieces

Seasoning

½ tsp salt

1½ tsps sugar

½ tsp monosodium glutamate (optional)

1 tsp dark soy sauce

2 tsps light soy sauce

1 tsp rice wine or dry sherry

2 tsps malt vinegar

1 tsp sesame oil

2 tsps cornflour

Oil for deep frying

1-2 red or green chillies, chopped

1.25cm/½-inch fresh root ginger, peeled and finely chopped

5cm/2 inches dried tangerine peel, coarsely ground or crumbled

2 spring onions, finely chopped

Sauce

½ tsp cornflour

1-2 tbsps water or stock

1. Mix the chicken pieces with the seasoning ingredients and stir well. Leave to marinate for 10-15 minutes. Remove the chicken pieces and reserve the marinade.

2. Heat a wok and add the oil for deep frying. Heat to 180°C/350°F, add the chicken pieces and fry for 4-5 minutes until golden. Drain chicken on kitchen paper and keep hot.

3. Allow the oil to cool then pour off, leaving 1 tbsp oil in the wok. Stir-fry the chillies, ginger, tangerine peel and spring onion for 2-3 minutes. When they begin to colour add the chicken and stir-fry for 1 minute.

4. Mix the reserved marinade with the sauce ingredients and pour over the chicken. Stir and cook for 2-3 minutes until the sauce thickens and the chicken is tender. Serve immediately.

TIME: Preparation takes 20 minutes including marinating time, cooking takes 15-20 minutes.

PREPARATION: Cook the chicken in batches.

COOK'S TIP: Have all the ingredients ready prepared before starting to cook.

CHICKEN WITH BEAN SPROUTS

Marinated chicken, stir-fried with bean sprouts and served with a sauce based on the marinade.

SERVES 4

4 boneless chicken breasts, skinned
1 tbsp Chinese wine
2 tsps cornflour
120g/4oz bean sprouts
2 tbsps oil
2 spring onions, finely sliced
1 tsp sugar
280ml/½ pint chicken stock
Salt and pepper

1. Cut the chicken into thin slices or strips.

2. Place the chicken on a plate and pour over the Chinese wine.

3. Sprinkle over the cornflour and stir together well. Leave to marinate for 30 minutes.

4. Blanch the bean sprouts in boiling, lightly salted water for 1 minute. Rinse under cold running water and set aside to drain.

5. Remove the chicken from the marinade with a slotted spoon. Heat the oil in a wok and stir-fry the spring onions and the chicken for 2-3 minutes.

6. Add the drained bean sprouts and the sugar. Stir in the marinade and the stock. Allow to heat through. Check the seasoning, adding salt and pepper to taste. Serve immediately.

TIME: Preparation takes about 20 minutes, marinating takes 30 minutes and cooking takes approximately 8-10 minutes.

VARIATION: Use half a small ordinary onion if spring onions are not available.

WATCHPOINT: As soon as you add the marinade to the wok, the mixture will thicken so have the stock ready to pour in immediately and stir continuously until all the ingredients have been fully incorporated.

CHICKEN AND SAUSAGE RISOTTO

This is really a one pot meal and one you won't have to cook in the oven.

SERVES 4-6

1.5kg/3lbs chicken portions, skinned, boned, and cut into cubes
45g/1½oz butter or margarine
1 large onion, roughly chopped
3 sticks celery, roughly chopped
1 large green pepper, roughly chopped
1 clove garlic, crushed
Salt and pepper
225g/8oz uncooked rice
400g/14oz canned tomatoes
180g/6oz smoked sausage, cut into 1.25cm/ ½-inch dice
850ml/1½ pints chicken stock
Chopped parsley

1. Use the chicken skin and bones and the onion and celery trimmings to make stock. Cover the ingredients with water, bring to the boil and then simmer slowly for 1 hour. Strain and reserve.

2. Melt the butter or margarine in a large saucepan and add the onion. Cook slowly to brown and then add the celery, green pepper and garlic and cook briefly.

3. Add the salt and pepper and the rice, stirring to mix well.

4. Add the chicken, tomatoes, sausage and stock and mix well. Bring to the boil, then reduce the heat to simmering and cook for about 20-25 minutes, stirring occasionally, until the chicken is done and the rice is tender. The rice should have absorbed most of the liquid by the time it has cooked. Sprinkle in the chopped parsley to serve.

TIME: Preparation takes about 1 hour and cooking takes about 30-35 minutes.

PREPARATION: Check the level of liquid occasionally as the rice is cooking and add more water or stock as necessary. If there is a lot of liquid left and the rice is nearly cooked, uncover the pan and boil rapidly.

SERVING IDEAS: Add a green salad to make a complete meal.

CHICKEN IN HOT PEPPER SAUCE

Stir-fried chicken served with peppers in a hot sauce.

SERVES 4

4 boned chicken breasts, skinned
2 tbsps oil
1 tsp chopped garlic
1 green pepper, cut into thin strips
1 red pepper, cut into thin strips
1 tsp wine vinegar
1 tbsp light soy sauce
1 tsp sugar
340ml/12 fl oz chicken stock
1 tbsp chilli sauce
2 tsps cornflour
Salt and pepper

1. Cut the chicken breasts crosswise into thin strips.

2. Heat the oil in a wok and stir-fry the garlic, chicken and the green and red peppers for 3-4 minutes.

3. Pour off any excess oil and deglaze the wok with the vinegar. Stir in the soy sauce, sugar and stock.

4. Gradually stir in the chilli sauce, tasting after each addition. Season with a little salt and pepper to taste.

5. Blend the cornflour with a little water and stir into the wok. Bring to the boil then simmer for 2-3 minutes. Serve piping hot.

TIME: Preparation takes 10 minutes and cooking takes approximately 10 minutes.

COOK'S TIP: Have all your ingredients ready prepared and measured out before you start to cook.

SERVING IDEAS: Serve with boiled or egg fried rice, on its own or as part of a Chinese meal.

CHICKEN IN SWEET-SOUR SAUCE

This is an Italian sweet and sour recipe which tastes just as good as the more common Chinese sweet-sour.

SERVES 4-6

1kg/2¼lbs chicken joints
1 large onion, chopped
1 large carrot, chopped
75ml/5 tbsps maraschino liqueur
75ml/5 tbsps white wine vinegar
140ml/¼ pint water
1 bay leaf
15 juniper berries
60ml/4 tbsps olive oil
Salt and pepper

1. Marinate the chicken joints for 4-6 hours in the chopped onion, carrot, liqueur, vinegar, and water, juniper berries and bay leaf.

2. Take the joints from the marinade and drain well, reserving the marinade. Sauté the joints in the olive oil until golden.

3. Place the joints in a shallow casserole, add the unstrained marinade, cover and cook at 180°C/350°F/Gas Mark 4 for about 1 hour or until the chicken is tender. Place on a warmed serving platter and keep warm.

4. Remove the bay leaf and press the cooking juices through a sieve. Reheat gently and pour over the chicken to serve.

TIME: Allow 4-6 hours for the chicken to marinate. Cooking takes about 1 hour.

SERVING IDEAS: Accompany with pasta and an Italian bread such as Ciabatta.

CHICKEN WITH RED PEPPERS

Easy as this recipe is, it looks and tastes good enough for guests.

SERVES 4

4 large red peppers
4 skinned and boned chicken breasts
1½ tbsps oil
Salt and pepper
1 clove garlic, finely chopped
3 tbsps white wine vinegar
2 spring onions, finely chopped
Sage leaves for garnish

1. Cut the peppers in half and remove the stems, cores and seeds. Flatten the peppers with the palm of your hand and brush the skin sides lightly with oil.

2. Place the peppers skin side up on the rack of a preheated grill and cook about 5cm/2 inches away from the heat source until the skins are well blistered and charred.

3. Seal the peppers in a thick plastic bag and allow them to stand until cool. Peel off the skins with a small vegetable knife. Cut peppers into thin strips and set aside.

4. Place the chicken breasts between two sheets of dampened greaseproof paper and flatten by hitting with a rolling pin or meat mallet.

5. Heat the oil in a large frying pan. Season the chicken breasts on both sides and add to the pan. Cook for 5 minutes, turn over and cook until tender, lightly browned and cooked through. Remove the chicken and keep it warm.

6. Add the pepper strips, garlic, vinegar and spring onions to the pan and cook briefly until the vinegar loses its strong aroma.

7. Place the chicken breasts on serving plates. Spoon over the pan juices.

8. Arrange the pepper mixture with the chicken and garnish with the sage leaves.

TIME: Preparation takes about 35-40 minutes and cooking takes about 10 minutes to char the peppers and about 15 minutes to finish the dish.

VARIATIONS: For convenience, the dish may be prepared with canned pimento instead of red peppers. These will be softer so cook the garlic, vinegar and onions to soften, and then add pimento.

BUYING GUIDE: If fresh sage is unavailable substitute coriander or parsley leaves as a garnish.

CHICKEN AND PANCETTA ROLLS

These rolls can be prepared in advance and kept chilled until cooking time. They make perfect dinner party fare.

SERVES 4

---

4 large chicken breasts, skinned
90g/3oz butter, softened
1 clove garlic, crushed
1 tbsp fresh oregano leaves or 1 tsp dried
    oregano
Salt and pepper
16 slices pancetta or prosciutto ham
Oil

---

1. Place each chicken breast between two sheets of damp greaseproof paper and bat out each piece with a rolling pin or meat mallet to flatten.

2. Mix the butter, garlic, oregano, salt and pepper together. Spread half of the mixture over each chicken escalope, then lay 4 slices of pancetta on top of each. Roll up, tucking in the sides and secure with cocktail sticks. Spread the remaining butter on the outside of each roll.

3. Cook the rolls under a medium hot preheated grill, for about 15-20 minutes, turning occasionally, until tender. Slice each roll into 1.25cm/½-inch rounds to serve.

TIME: Preparation takes about 20 minutes and cooking takes 15-20 minutes.

VARIATION: The chicken rolls can be sautéed in a frying pan.

SERVING IDEAS: Serve with a fresh tomato sauce, and accompany with rice or new potatoes and French beans.

BLUE STILTON CHICKEN

These chicken parcels make a lovely and unusual dish for a dinner party.

SERVES 4

120g/4oz Blue Stilton (or Danish Blue)
    cheese
90g/3oz butter
2 tbsps double cream
1 tbsp parsley, finely chopped
4 chicken breasts, skinned, boned and
    beaten flat
8 rashers bacon
2 tbsps oil
30g/1oz butter
140ml/¼ pint dry white wine
140ml/¼ pint chicken stock
Salt and pepper
2 tsps cornflour

---

1. In a bowl, cream together the cheese and butter then add the cream to make a spreading consistency. Add the parsley.

2. Spread the cheese mixture on one side only of the chicken breasts, leaving a narrow border. Roll the breasts up, wrap each one in 2 bacon rashers and secure with a cocktail stick or skewer.

3. In a flameproof casserole, heat the oil and butter together and, when sizzling, brown the chicken parcels on each side until golden.

4. Pour in the wine, chicken stock and seasoning (go gently with the salt because the cheese stuffing will be quite salty). Bring to the boil, cover and simmer gently for about 40 minutes, turning occasionally.

5. When cooked, remove the chicken to a hot serving dish and take out the sticks or skewers.

6. Blend the cornflour in a cup with a little cold water and add to the pan juices. Stir until the sauce thickens, adjust seasoning if necessary and pour over the chicken. Serve at once.

TIME: Preparation takes about 25 minutes and cooking takes 45-50 minutes.

PREPARATION: The chicken parcels can be prepared in advance of cooking and kept refrigerated.

SERVING IDEAS: Serve with rice or new potatoes and broccoli.

CHICKEN WITH OLIVES

This is a chicken sauté dish for olive lovers. Use more or less of them as your own taste dictates.

SERVES 4-6

2 tbsps olive oil
30g/1oz butter or margarine
1 × 1.5kg/3lb chicken, jointed
1 clove garlic, crushed
140ml/¼ pint white wine
140ml/¼ pint chicken stock
Salt and pepper
4 courgettes, cut in 1.25cm/½-inch pieces
20 pitted black and green olives
2 tbsps chopped parsley

1. Heat the oil in a large frying pan and add the butter or margarine. When foaming, add the chicken skin side down in one layer. Brown one side of the chicken and turn over to brown the other side. Cook the chicken in two batches if necessary.

2. Turn the chicken skin side up and add the garlic, wine, stock, salt and pepper. Bring to the boil, cover the pan and allow to simmer over a gentle heat for about 30-35 minutes.

3. Add the courgettes and cook for 10 minutes. Once the chicken and courgettes are done, add the olives and cook to heat through. Add the parsley and remove to a dish to serve.

TIME: Preparation takes about 25 minutes, cooking takes about 50-55 minutes.

SERVING IDEAS: Serve with rice or pasta and tomato salad.

VARIATION: Artichoke hearts may be used in place of the courgettes.

POACHED CHICKEN WITH CREAM SAUCE

Poaching chicken keeps it tender and succulent.

SERVES 4

1 × 2kg/4½lb whole chicken
8-10 celery sticks, tops reserved
120g/4oz thickly sliced streaky bacon
2 cloves garlic, crushed
1 large onion, stuck with 4 cloves
1 bay leaf
1 sprig fresh thyme
Salt and pepper
Water to cover
90g/3oz butter or margarine
45g/6 tbsps flour
280ml/½ pint single cream

1. Remove the fat from just inside the cavity of the chicken. Singe any pin feathers over a gas flame or pull them out with tweezers.

2. Tie the chicken legs together and tuck the wing tips under the body to hold the neck flap. Place the chicken in a large casserole or stock pot. Chop the celery tops and add to the pot. Place the bacon over the chicken and add the garlic, onion with the cloves, bay leaf, sprig of thyme, salt, pepper and water to cover.

3. Bring to the boil, reduce the heat and simmer gently, covered, for 50 minutes or until the chicken is just tender.

4. Cut the celery into 7.5cm/3-inch lengths and add to the chicken. Simmer a further 20 minutes, or until the celery is just tender.

5. Remove the chicken to a serving plate and keep warm. Strain the stock and reserve the bacon and celery pieces. Skim fat off the top of the stock and add enough water to make up 570ml/1 pint, if necessary.

6. Melt 15g/½oz of the butter or margarine in the casserole and sauté the bacon until just crisp. Drain on kitchen paper and roughly crumble.

7. Melt the rest of the butter in the casserole or pan and when foaming, take off the heat. Stir in the flour and gradually add the chicken stock. Add the cream and bring to the boil, stirring constantly. Simmer until the mixture is thickened.

8. Untie the legs and trim the leg ends. If wished, remove the skin from the chicken and coat with the sauce. Garnish with the bacon and the reserved celery pieces.

TIME: Preparation takes about 10 minutes and cooking takes about 1½ hours.

SERVING IDEAS: The chicken may be jointed into 8 pieces before coating with sauce, if wished. Cut the leg joints in two, dividing the thigh and the drumstick. Cut the breast in two, leaving some white meat attached to the wings. Cut through any bones with scissors.

CHICKEN WITH MANGO

The exotic flavour of mango and spices make a lovely combination in this dish.

SERVES 4

2 tbsps oil
1 tsp grated ginger
½ tsp ground cinnamon
4 chicken breasts, cut into shreds
4 spring onions, sliced diagonally
1 tbsp light soy sauce
1 chicken stock cube
140ml/¼ pint water
1 tsp sugar
Salt and pepper
2 ripe mangoes, sliced, or 1 can sliced mangoes, drained

1. Heat a wok and add the oil. Add the ginger and cinnamon, and fry for 30 seconds.

2. Add the chicken and spring onions, and stir-fry for 5 minutes.

3. Add the light soy sauce, crumbled chicken stock cube, water and sugar, and bring to the boil.

4. Add salt and pepper to taste, and simmer for 15 minutes.

5. Add the mangoes and sherry, and simmer, uncovered, until sauce has reduced and thickened.

TIME: Preparation takes about 10 minutes and cooking takes about 30 minutes.

PREPARATION: To cut up a fresh mango first remove the peel then cut off the two rounded sides either side of the large flat stone.

SERVING IDEAS: Serve with boiled rice and mange tout peas.

POULET GRILLÉ AU LIMON

Crisp chicken with a tang of limes makes an elegant yet quickly-made entrée.
From the warm regions of southern France, it is perfect for a summer meal.

SERVES 4

2 × 900g/2lb chickens
1 tsp basil
90ml/6 tbsps olive oil
4 limes
Salt, pepper and sugar

1. Remove the leg ends, neck and wing tips from the chicken and discard them.

2. Split the chickens in half, cutting away the backbone completely and discarding it.

3. Loosen the ball and socket joint in the leg and flatten each half of the chicken by hitting it with the flat side of a cleaver.

4. Season the chicken on both sides with salt and pepper and sprinkle over the basil. Place the chicken in a shallow dish and pour over 2 tbsps of olive oil. Squeeze the juice from 2 of the limes over the chicken.

Cover and leave to marinate in the refrigerator for 4 hours or overnight.

5. Heat the grill to its highest setting and preheat the oven to 190°C/375°F/Gas Mark 5. Remove the chicken from the marinade and place in the grill pan. Cook one side until golden brown and turn the pieces over. Sprinkle with 1 tbsp olive oil and brown the other side.

6. Place the chicken in a roasting pan, sprinkle with the remaining oil and roast in the oven for about 25 minutes. Cut the peel from the remaining limes, removing all the pith, and slice them thinly. When the chicken is cooked, place the lime slices on top and sprinkle lightly with sugar. Place under the grill for a few minutes to caramelise the sugar and cook the limes. Place in a serving dish and spoon over any remaining marinade and the cooking juices. Serve immediately.

TIME: Preparation takes about 25 minutes, plus 4 hours marinating, cooking takes about 35 minutes.

WATCHPOINT: Sugar will burn and turn bitter quickly, so watch carefully while grilling.

VARIATIONS: If limes are too expensive, use lemons instead. Vary the choice of herb.

Chicken and Avocado Salad

The creamy herb dressing complements this easy summer salad.

SERVES 4

8 anchovy fillets, soaked in milk, rinsed and dried

1 spring onion, chopped

2 tbsps chopped fresh tarragon

3 tbsps chopped chives

30g/4 tbsps chopped parsley

280ml/½ pint mayonnaise

140ml/¼ pint natural yogurt

2 tbsps tarragon vinegar

Pinch sugar and cayenne pepper

1 large head lettuce

450g/1lb cooked chicken

1 avocado, peeled and sliced or cubed coated with 1 tbsp lemon juice

1. Combine all the ingredients, except the lettuce, chicken and avocado in a food processor. Work the ingredients until smooth, and well mixed. Leave in the refrigerator at least 1 hour for the flavours to blend.

2. Shred the lettuce or tear into bite-size pieces and arrange on plates.

3. Top the lettuce with the cooked chicken cut into strips or cubes.

4. Spoon the dressing over the chicken and garnish the salad with the avocado. Serve any remaining dressing separately.

TIME: Preparation takes about 30 minutes plus 1 hour refrigeration for the dressing.

PREPARATION: Dressing may be prepared ahead of time and kept in the refrigerator for a day or two.

POULET FRICASSÉE

This is a white stew, enriched and thickened with an egg and cream mixture which is called a liaison.

SERVES 4

60g/2oz butter or margarine
1 × 1.5kg/3lb chicken, quartered and
    skinned
30g/1oz flour
570ml/1 pint chicken stock
Grated rind and juice of ½ lemon
1 bouquet garni
12-16 small onions, peeled
340g/12oz button mushrooms, whole if
    small, quartered if large
2 egg yolks
90ml/6 tbsps double cream
3 tbsps milk (optional)
Salt and pepper
2 tbsps chopped parsley and thyme
Lemon slices to garnish

1. Melt 45g/1½oz of the butter in a large frying pan. Place in the chicken in one layer and cook over gentle heat for about 5 minutes, or until the chicken is no longer pink. Do not allow the chicken to brown. If necessary, cook the chicken in two batches. When the chicken is sufficiently cooked, remove it from the pan and set aside.

2. Stir the flour into the butter remaining in the pan and cook over very low heat, stirring continuously for about 1 minute, or until pale straw in colour. Remove the pan from the heat and gradually beat in the chicken stock. When blended smoothly, add lemon rind and juice, return the pan to the heat and bring to the boil, whisking constantly. Reduce the heat and allow the sauce to simmer for 1 minute.

3. Return the chicken to the pan with any juices that have accumulated and add the bouquet garni. The sauce should almost cover the chicken. If it does not, add more stock or water. Bring to the boil, cover the pan and reduce the heat. Allow the chicken to simmer gently for 30 minutes.

4. Meanwhile, melt the remaining butter in a small frying pan, add the onions, cover and cook very gently for 10 minutes. Do not allow the onions to brown. Remove the onions from the pan with a draining spoon and add to the chicken. Cook the mushrooms in the remaining butter for 2 minutes. Set the mushrooms aside and add them to the chicken 10 minutes before the end of cooking.

5. Test the chicken by piercing a thigh portion with a sharp knife. If the juices run clear, the chicken is cooked. Transfer chicken and vegetables to a serving plate and discard the bouquet garni. Skim the sauce of any fat and boil it rapidly to reduce by almost half.

6. Blend the egg yolks and cream together and whisk-in several spoonfuls of the hot sauce. Return the egg yolk and cream mixture to the remaining sauce and cook gently for 2-3 minutes. Stir the sauce constantly and do not allow it to boil. If very thick, add milk. Adjust the seasoning, stir in the parsley and thyme and spoon over the chicken in a serving dish. Garnish with lemon slices.

PECAN CHICKEN

Pecans can be used in both sweet and savoury dishes. Here, their rich, sweet taste complements a stuffing for chicken.

SERVES 4

4 boned chicken breasts
45g/1½oz butter or margarine
1 small onion, finely chopped
90g/3oz pork sausage meat
90g/3oz fresh breadcrumbs
1 tsp chopped thyme
1 tsp chopped parsley
1 small egg, lightly beaten
120g/4oz pecan halves
280ml/½ pint chicken stock
1 tbsp flour
2 tbsps sherry
Salt and pepper
Chopped parsley or 1 bunch watercress to
    garnish

1. Cut a small pocket in the thick side of each chicken breast using a small knife.

2. Melt 15g/½oz of the butter in a small saucepan and add the onion. Cook for a few minutes over gentle heat to soften. Add the sausage meat and turn up the heat to brown. Break up the sausage meat with a fork as it cooks.

3. Drain off any excess fat and add the breadcrumbs, herbs and a pinch of salt and pepper. Allow to cool slightly and add enough egg to hold the mixture together. Chop the pecans, reserving 8, and add to the stuffing.

4. Using a small teaspoon, fill the pocket in each chicken breast with some of the stuffing.

5. Melt another 15g/½oz of the butter in a casserole and place in the chicken breasts, skin side down first. Brown over moderate heat and turn over. Brown the other side quickly to seal.

6. Pour in the stock, cover the casserole and cook for about 25-30 minutes in a preheated 180°C/350°F/Gas Mark 4 oven until tender.

7. When the chicken is cooked, remove it to a serving plate to keep warm. Reserve the cooking liquid.

8. Melt the remaining butter in a small saucepan and stir in the flour. Cook to a pale straw colour. Strain on the cooking liquid and add the sherry. Bring to the boil and stir constantly until thickened. Add the reserved pecans and seasoning.

9. Spoon some of the sauce over the chicken. Garnish with chopped parsley or a bunch of watercress.

TIME: Preparation takes about 30 minutes and cooking takes about 40 minutes.

VARIATION: If pecans are unavailable, use hazelnuts. Crush the hazelnuts roughly for the garnish and brown lightly in the butter before adding flour for the sauce.

SERVING IDEAS: Serve with a rice or sauté potatoes.

Poulet Sauté Vallée d'Auge

This dish contains all the ingredients that Normandy is famous for – butter, cream, apples and Calvados.

SERVES 4

60g/2oz butter or margarine

2 tbsps oil

1 × 1.5kg/3lb chicken, cut into eight portions

60ml/4 tbsps Calvados

90ml/6 tbsps chicken stock

2 apples, peeled, cored and coarsely chopped

1 shallot, finely chopped

2 sticks celery, finely chopped

½ tsp dried thyme, crumbled

2 egg yolks, lightly beaten

90ml/6 tbsps double cream

Salt and white pepper

Garnish

30g/1oz butter

2 apples, quartered, cored and cut into cubes

Sugar

1 bunch watercress or small parsley sprigs

1. Heat half the butter and all of the oil in a large frying pan over moderate heat. When the foam begins to subside, brown the chicken, a few pieces at a time, skin side down first. When all the chicken is browned, pour off most of the fat from the pan and return the chicken to the pan.

2. Pour the Calvados into a small saucepan and warm over gentle heat. Ignite with a match and pour, while still flaming, over the chicken. Shake the frying pan gently until the flames subside. If the Calvados should flare up, cover the pan immediately with the lid.

3. Pour over the stock and scrape any browned chicken juices from the bottom of the pan. Set the chicken aside.

4. Melt the remaining butter in a small saucepan or frying pan. Cook the chopped apples, shallot and celery and the thyme for about 10 minutes or until soft but not brown.

5. Spoon over the chicken and return the pan to the high heat. Bring to the boil, then reduce heat, cover the pan and simmer for 50 minutes.

6. When the chicken is cooked, beat the eggs and cream. With a whisk, gradually beat in some of the hot sauce. Pour the mixture back into a saucepan and cook over a low heat for 2-3 minutes, stirring constantly until the sauce thickens and coats the back of a spoon.

7. Season the sauce with salt and white pepper and set aside while preparing the garnish.

8. Put the butter in a small frying pan and when foaming, add the apple. Toss over a high heat until beginning to soften. Sprinkle with sugar and cook until the apple begins to caramelise.

9. To serve, coat the chicken with the sauce and decorate with watercress or parsley. Spoon the caramelised apples over the chicken.

Spring Chickens with Bitter Chocolate Sauce

A small amount of unsweetened chocolate lends a rich depth of colour and a delightfully mysterious flavour to a savoury sauce.

SERVES 4

60ml/4 tbsps olive oil
4 single (small) poussins
Salt and pepper
3 tbsps flour
1 clove garlic, crushed
280ml/½ pint chicken stock
60ml/4 tbsps dry white wine
2 tsps unsweetened cooking chocolate, grated
Lemon slices to garnish

1. Heat the oil in a heavy-based pan or casserole. Season the poussins and place them, breast side down first, in the hot oil. Cook until golden brown on all sides, turning frequently.

2. Transfer the poussins to a plate and add the flour to the casserole. Cook to a pale straw colour.

3. Add the garlic and cook to soften. Pour on the stock gradually, stirring well. Add the wine and bring to the boil.

4. Reduce to simmering, replace the poussins and cover the casserole. Cook for 20-30 minutes, or until the poussins are tender.

5. Transfer the cooked poussins to a serving dish and skim any fat from the surface of the sauce. Add the grated chocolate and cook, stirring quickly, over a low heat for 2-3 minutes. Pour some of the sauce over the poussins and garnish with lemon slices. Serve the rest of the sauce separately.

TIME: Preparation takes about 10 minutes, cooking takes about 35-45 minutes.

BUYING GUIDE: Unsweetened cooking chocolate is not the same as plain chocolate, which must not be used as a substitute. Unsweetened chocolate is available in large supermarkets and speciality shops.

SERVING IDEAS: Serve with rice and a vegetable such as peas or asparagus, or with a green salad.

TARRAGON CHICKEN PANCAKES

These attractive pancakes look sophisticated enough for a dinner party, but are so easy to make, you can indulge yourself at any time.

SERVES 4

120g/4oz plain wholemeal flour
1 egg
280ml/½ pint milk
Oil for frying
45g/1½oz butter
3 tbsps plain flour
280ml/½ pint milk
Salt and black pepper, to taste
225g/8oz cooked chicken, chopped
1 avocado pear, peeled, halved, stoned and
    chopped
2 tsps lemon juice
1 tbsp chopped fresh tarragon

1. Put the wholemeal flour into a large bowl, and make a slight well in the centre. Break the egg into the well and begin to beat the egg carefully into the flour, incorporating only a little flour at a time.

2. Add the milk gradually to the egg and flour mixture, beating well between additions, until all the milk is incorporated and the batter is smooth.

3. Heat a little oil in a small frying pan, or crêpe pan, and cook about 2 tbsps of the batter at a time, tipping and rotating the pan, so that the batter spreads evenly over the base to form a pancake. Flip the pancake over, to cook the second side.

4. Repeat this process until all the batter has been used up. Keep the pancakes warm, until required.

5. Melt the butter in a small saucepan, stir in the flour and cook over a medium heat for 1-2 minutes. Remove from the heat and gradually stir in the milk. Bring to the boil, stirring, then simmer for 1-2 minutes. Season to taste.

6. Stir the chopped chicken, avocado, lemon juice and tarragon into the sauce.

7. Fold each pancake in half, and then in half again, to form a triangle.

8. Carefully open part of the triangle out to form an envelope, and fill this with the chicken and avocado mixture.

TIME: Preparation takes about 25 minutes, and cooking takes about 25 minutes.

SERVING IDEAS: Serve piping hot, garnished with watercress and accompany with a crisp green salad.

POUSSINS IN A CURRY SAUCE

Whole roast poussins served with a spicy sauce makes a nice alternative to the usual curry.

SERVES 4

60g/2oz butter
1 tsp oil
4 small poussins
1 medium onion, finely chopped
1 clove garlic, crushed
2 tsps curry powder
140ml/¼ pint chicken stock
Squeeze of lemon juice
2 tsps mango chutney
30g/1oz sultanas
1 rounded tsp cornflour
Cold water

---

1. Put butter and the oil in a roasting tin and put into an oven preheated to 180°C/350°F/ Gas Mark 4. When sizzling, remove from the oven, add the poussins and baste well.

Return the tin to the oven and roast the birds for about 35 minutes, basting at regular intervals until they are cooked. Test with a skewer inserted into the thickest part of the leg. If the liquid runs clear, the poussins are cooked. Remove from the roasting tin and keep them warm.

2. Drain off any excess fat from the tin and place it over a medium heat. Add the chopped onion and garlic and sauté for a few minutes until softened. Reduce the heat, add the curry powder and stir well for 2-3 minutes. Pour in the chicken stock and stir until it is bubbling. Add the squeeze of lemon juice, chutney and sultanas.

3. In a cup, blend the cornflour with a little cold water and add it to the sauce. Mix well and cook for a few more minutes. Pour over the poussins or serve separately.

TIME: Preparation takes about 10 minutes and cooking takes about 40 minutes.

VARIATION: Substitute lime pickle for mango chutney for a different flavour.

SERVING IDEAS: Serve with poppadums and rice.

Niçoise Chicken

The combination of fresh herbs, tomatoes and black olives brings the taste of Provence to your table.

SERVES 4

4 boned chicken breasts, unskinned
4 tbsps oil
2 tbsps lemon juice

Tapenade filling
450g/1lb large black olives, pitted
2 tbsps capers
1 clove garlic, roughly chopped
4 anchovy fillets
2 tbsps olive oil

Raw tomato sauce
450g/1lb ripe tomatoes, skinned, seeded
    and chopped
1 shallot, very finely chopped
2 tbsps chopped parsley
2 tbsps chopped basil
2 tbsps white wine vinegar
2 tbsps olive oil
1 tbsp sugar
Salt and pepper
1 tbsp tomato purée (optional)

1. Cut a pocket in the thickest side of the chicken breasts.

2. Combine half the olives, half the capers and the remaining ingredients for the tapenade in a blender or food processor. Work to a purée.

3. Add the remaining olives and capers and process a few times to chop them roughly.

4. Fill the chicken breasts with the tapenade. Chill to help filling to firm.

5. Baste the skin side with the oil and lemon juice mixed together. Cook skin side down first for 10 minutes under a preheated medium hot grill. Turn over, baste again and grill for another 10 minutes on the other side or until tender.

6. Meanwhile, combine the tomato sauce ingredients and mix very well. Serve with the chicken.

TIME: Preparation takes about 30 minutes and cooking takes about 20 minutes.

PREPARATION: Both the filling and sauce can be made in advance and kept refrigerated.

SERVING IDEAS: Serve with new potatoes and fine green beans.

POUSSINS ESPAGNOLE

The olive oil in this recipe gives a wonderful flavour to the sauce.

SERVES 4

4 single (small) poussins
Salt and freshly ground black pepper
Olive oil, to brush
4 small wedges of lime or lemon
4 bay leaves
2 tbsps olive oil
1 small onion, thinly sliced
1 clove garlic, crushed
450g/1lb tomatoes
140ml/¼ pint red wine
140ml/¼ pint chicken or vegetable stock
1 tbsp tomato purée
1 green chilli, seeded and thinly sliced
1 small red pepper, cut into thin strips
1 small green pepper, cut into thin strips
2 tbsps chopped, blanched almonds
1 tbsp pine kernels
12 small black olives, pitted
1 tbsp raisins

1. Rub the poussins inside and out with salt and pepper. Brush the skins with olive oil and push a wedge of lemon or lime, and a bay leaf into the cavity of each one.

2. Roast the poussins, uncovered, in a pre-heated oven 190°C/375°F/Gas Mark 5 for 45 minutes, or until just tender.

3. Meanwhile, heat the 2 tbsps olive oil in a large frying pan and gently cook the onion and the garlic until they are soft, but not coloured.

4. Cut a slit into the skins of each tomato and plunge into boiling water for 30 seconds.

5. Using a sharp knife carefully peel away the skins from the blanched tomatoes.

6. Chop the tomatoes roughly. Remove and discard the seeds and cores.

7. Add the chopped tomatoes to the cooked onion and garlic, and fry gently for a further 2 minutes.

8. Add all the remaining ingredients and simmer for 10-15 minutes, or until the tomatoes have completely softened and the sauce has thickened slightly.

9. Arrange the poussins on a serving dish and spoon a little of the sauce over each one.

10. Serve hot with the remaining sauce in a separate jug.

TIME: Preparation takes 15 minutes, cooking takes about 45 minutes.

SERVING IDEAS: Serve with rice and a mixed green salad.

COOK'S TIP: If the poussins start to get too brown during the cooking time, cover them with aluminium foil.

CHICKEN MARENGO

This classic dish uses expensive ingredients so save it for a special occasion.

SERVES 6

6 chicken portions
Salt and pepper
60g/2oz butter
175ml/6 fl oz olive oil
4 ripe tomatoes, skinned and sieved
1 clove garlic, chopped
6 sprigs parsley (chop 5 sprigs)
420ml/¾ pint dry white wine
225g/8oz fresh wild ceps or 45g/1½oz
    dried wild mushrooms
1 small white truffle or black truffle, sliced
1 small onion, sliced
1 bay leaf
1 stick celery, chopped
Pinch of thyme
Peppercorns
6 raw king prawns
6 slices sandwich bread, crusts trimmed
6 eggs

1. Wash the chicken and pat dry with kitchen paper. Sprinkle with salt and pepper.

2. Heat 15g/½oz of the butter and 90ml/6 tbsps of the oil in a large frying pan and brown the pieces of chicken, turning to get all sides browned.

3. Add the tomatoes, garlic and half the chopped parsley. Boil half of the wine for 2 minutes, add to the pan, cover and cook over moderate heat for 20 minutes.

4. Meanwhile, cut off the bottoms of the mushroom stems (if you are using fresh wild mushrooms), clean and slice. If using dried, soak for 30 minutes in warm water, then drain and chop.

5. Put 30g/1oz of the butter in a pan with 2 tbsps of the oil. Add the mushrooms and truffle slices to the pan. Sprinkle with salt and pepper and sauté until wilted. Before removing from the heat, sprinkle with the remaining chopped parsley.

6. Add the mushrooms to the chicken. Cover and simmer another 15-20 minutes or until the chicken is tender.

7. Meanwhile, heat the remaining wine in a saucepan. Add the onion, unchopped parsley sprig, bay leaf, celery, thyme, several peppercorns and 1/2 tsp salt. When the wine comes to the boil add the king prawns and simmer for 5 minutes; drain and reserve the prawns, then shell and de-vein.

8. Heat the remaining oil in a frying pan and fry bread slices until brown on both sides.

9. Heat the remaining butter in a large frying pan and fry the eggs until the whites are firm and the yolks still soft. Remove from the heat and place the fried eggs on the slices of bread.

10. Place the chicken in the centre of a large round serving dish. Spoon over the pan juices. Place the slices of bread with eggs around the edges, alternating with the king prawns.

TIME: Preparation takes 20 minutes, and cooking takes about 1 hour.

BUYING GUIDE: Dried ceps, or porcini to give them their Italian name, and jars of truffles are available from delicatessens and specialist food shops.

POUSSINS IN RED WINE

This dish, served with creamed potatoes and a green vegetable, is suitable for a winter supper or dinner party.

SERVES 4

1½ tbsps oil
6 rashers of streaky bacon, chopped
2 medium onions, finely chopped
4 single (small) poussins
280ml/½ pint chicken stock
280ml/½ pint red wine
1 bay leaf
1 scant tsp thyme
120g/4oz mushrooms, thinly sliced

1. In a large casserole, heat the oil and sauté the bacon until crisp. Using a slotted spoon, remove the bacon to a plate. Add the onion to the oil and cook until soft. Remove.

2. Add the poussins to the oil, turning frequently, until the skin is slightly crisp. Add the chicken stock and red wine so that the liquid almost covers the birds.

3. Add the cooked bacon and onion, the bay leaf, thyme and mushrooms and placing the poussins breast-side down, cook in an oven, preheated to 180°C/350°F/Gas Mark 4, for approximately 1½ hours. Test with a sharp knife. The meat should feel very tender. Remove the poussins to a warm serving dish.

4. To the sauce add a beurre manié of 2 tsps butter worked together on a plate with 2 tsps plain flour. Add in small pieces, beating well with a wooden spoon. This will thicken the sauce, some of which can be poured over the poussins. Serve the rest in a warm sauce boat.

TIME: Preparation takes 20 minutes and cooking takes 1 hour 35 minutes.

VARIATION: Use white wine for a change.